Jelly Roll Jazz

by Jean Ann Wright

Landauer Publishing, LLC

Jelly Roll Jazz

by Jean Ann Wright

Copyright © 2015 by Landauer Publishing, LLC
Projects Copyright © 2015
by Jean Ann Wright

This book was designed, produced,
and published by Landauer Publishing, LLC
3100 101st Street, Urbandale, IA 50322
515/287/2144   800/557/2144   landauerpub.com

President/Publisher: Jeramy Lanigan Landauer
Editor: Jeri Simon
Art Director: Laurel Albright
Photographer: Sue Voegtlin

ISBN 13: 978-1-935726-83-8
This book printed on acid-free paper.
Printed in United States

10-9-8-7-6-5-4-3-2-1

 FACEBOOK.COM/
LANDAUERPUBLISHING
  YOUTUBE.COM/
LANDAUERPUBLISHING
 PINTEREST.COM/
LANDAUERPUB

About the Author

Jean Ann Wright has been sewing and making quilts for over 25 years. She majored in textiles and fine arts at Palm Beach State College and has combined these two disciplines to become a fiber artist. From 1986 to 2006 she edited an international quilting magazine titled QUILT, plus a variety of special interest quilting titles with the same publishing company.

Jean Ann is the co-author of *Circle of Nine, Log Cabin Quilts The basics & beyond, Quilting a Circle of Nine* and *The Best of Circle of Nine*. She is the author of *Quilt Sashings & Settings, The basics & beyond, Jelly Roll Jambalaya* and is the designer of several specialty rulers from Creative Grids®.

PROJECTS

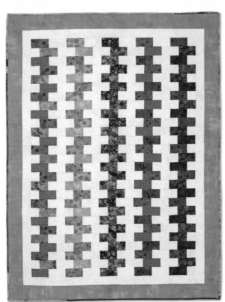

Bebop Stomp Quilt

6

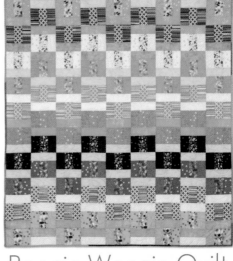

Boogie Woogie Quilt

10

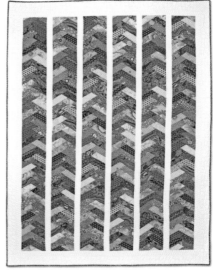

Color Fusion Quilt

14

Gypsy Jazz Quilt

18

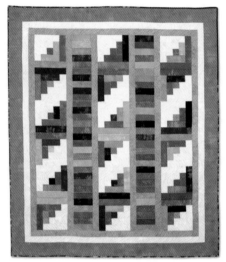

Let's Swing Quilt

24

Ragtime Quilt

28

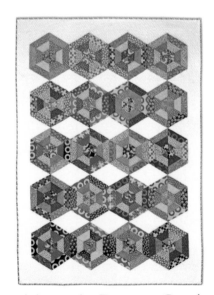

Hex-A-Dizzy Quilt

32

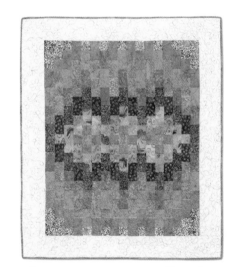

Syncopation Quilt

40

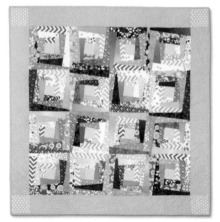

Pick Up Sticks Quilt

44

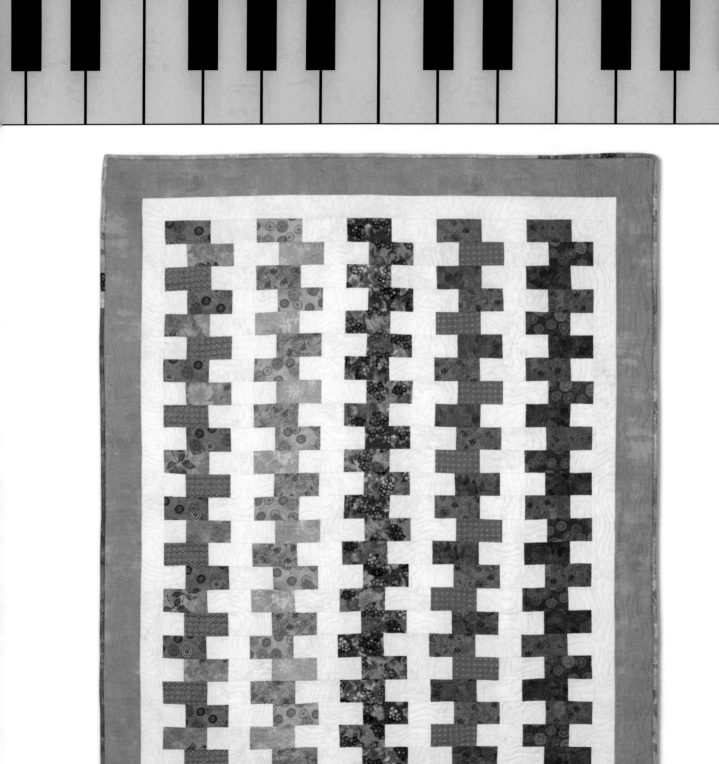

Quilt designed and pieced by Jean Ann Wright; longarm quilted by Alta Miele
Precut fabric bundle: Crush by Sue Zipkin for Clothworks

Finished quilt size: 50" x 66"
Precut bundle = 2-1/2" x WOF strips
WOF = Width of fabric
NOTE: Sew with a scant 1/4" seam allowance

Fabric Requirements

- 1 precut bundle of
  (20) 2-1/2" x WOF strips

- 1-1/2 yards ivory or light beige tonal
  background fabric

- 1 yard green fabric

- 3-1/4 yards backing fabric

- Twin-size batting

Cutting

Separate the precut strips into 5 color
groups with 3 strips in each group. Set
aside the remaining 5 strips for binding.

From **each** of the 15 precut strips, cut:

(9) 2-1/2" x 4-1/2" rectangles
    Stack each color group together.
    Save the leftover fabric pieces for
    the binding.

From ivory background fabric, cut:

(13) 2-1/2" x WOF strips
    From 1 of the strips, cut:
    (17) 2-1/2" squares
    From each remaining strip, cut:
    (9) 2-1/2" x 4-1/2" rectangles
    (1) 2-1/2" square

(6) 2-1/2" x WOF strips. Sew the strips
    together end-to-end and cut:
    (2) 2-1/2" x 54-1/2" side inner
        border strips
    (2) 2-1/2" x 42-1/2" top/bottom
        inner border strips

From green fabric, cut:

(6) 4-1/2" x WOF strips. Sew the strips
    together end-to-end and cut:
    (2) 4-1/2" x 58-1/2" side outer
        border strips
    (2) 4-1/2" x 50-1/2" top/bottom
        outer border strips

Bebop Stomp Quilt

The Bebop Stomp is a dance performed to a form of modern jazz popular in the 1940's known as bebop. Bebop is played at a fast tempo with improvisations based on a particular structure. The Tuscany-themed fabrics and the mental picture of stomping grapes to crush them into juice combined to create the featured quilt.

Quilt Center Assembly

1. Alternate the 3 prints in each color stack. Line up the color stacks in the order to be sewn.

2. Make a separate stack of 2-1/2" ivory squares and 2-1/2" x 4-1/2" ivory rectangles.

3. Referring to the Row Assembly Diagram, lay out the print and ivory pieces in 27 horizontal rows. The odd numbered rows begin with a 2-1/2" ivory square and end with a 2-1/2" x 4-1/2" print rectangle. Even numbered rows begin with a 2-1/2" x 4-1/2" print rectangle and end with a 2-1/2" ivory square.

4. Referring to the Quilt Center Assembly Diagram, sew the pieces together in rows. Press the seams toward the print rectangles.

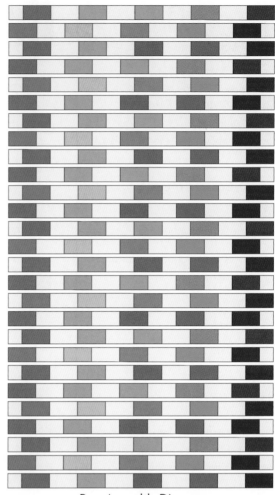

Row Assembly Diagram

5. Sew the rows together to complete the quilt center. Press seams as each row is added. The jagged vertical rows will appear as each row is added.

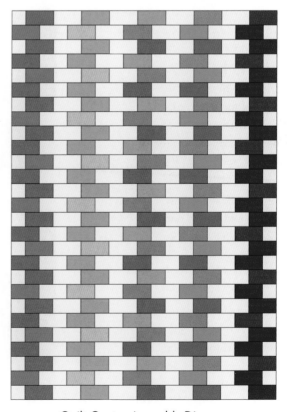

Quilt Center Assembly Diagram

Adding the Borders

1. Sew the 2-1/2" x 54-1/2" ivory side inner border strips to opposite sides of the quilt center. Sew the 2-1/2" x 42-1/2" ivory top/bottom inner border strips to the top/bottom of the quilt center. Press seams toward borders.

2. Sew the 4-1/2" x 58-1/2" side outer border strips to opposite sides of the quilt center. Sew the 4-1/2" x 50-1/2" top/bottom outer border strips to the top/bottom of the quilt center. Press seams toward borders to complete the quilt top.

Finishing

1. Layer the quilt top, batting and backing.

2. Baste the layers together. Hand or machine quilt as desired. The featured quilt was quilted using a slightly square spiral design going up and down the vertical rows of color to emphasize each row.

3. Sew (5) 2-1/2" x WOF precut strips and leftover fabric from the 2-1/2" x 4-1/2" rectangles together along the short edges to make one continuous binding strip. Press seams open.

4. Press the strip in half lengthwise, wrong sides together, and sew to the raw edge of the quilt top. Fold binding over raw edges and hand stitch in place.

Quilt designed and pieced by Jean Ann Wright; longarm quilted by Sue Bentley
Longarm quilting design: Chinook by Denise Schillinger
Jelly Roll bundle: Barcelona by Zen Chic for Moda
Additional fabric: Grunge by BasicGrey for Moda

Boogie Woogie Quilt

Finished quilt size: 54" x 62"
Jelly Roll bundle = 2-1/2" x WOF strips
WOF = Width of fabric
NOTE: Sew with a scant 1/4" seam allowance

Boogie woogie became popular during the late 1920's and was mainly associated with dancing. It started as a solo piano style but eventually included guitar, big band, country western and gospel. The blocks in the Boogie Woogie quilt resemble piano keys and the rows of this quilt are arranged to move up and down as they dance along in musical rows.

Fabric Requirements

- 1 jelly roll bundle of
  (40) 2-1/2" x WOF strips

- 1/2 yard lime green fabric

- 1/2 yard orange fabric

- 1/2 yard white fabric

- 1/4 yard teal fabric

- 3-1/2 yards backing fabric

- Twin-size batting

Cutting

Separate the precut strips into 10 color groups with 3 strips in each group. Set aside 7 remaining strips for binding.

From lime green fabric, cut:
(6) 2-1/2" x WOF strips
　　From the strips, cut:
　　(36) 2-1/2" x 6-1/2" spacers

From orange fabric, cut:
(5) 2-1/2" x WOF strips
　　From the strips, cut:
　　(27) 2-1/2" x 6-1/2" spacers

From white fabric, cut:
(5) 2-1/2" x WOF strips
　　From the strips, cut:
　　(27) 2-1/2" x 6-1/2" spacers
　　Set 9 aside for end spacers.

From teal fabric, cut:
(2) 2-1/2" x WOF strips
　　From the strips, cut:
　　(9) 2-1/2" x 6-1/2" spacers

Block Assembly

1. Sew the strips in each color group together along the long edges to make a strip set. Press seams. Make a total of 10 strip sets.

2. Cut the strip sets into 4-1/2" segments. You will be able to cut 9 segments from each strip set for a total of 90 segments. Keep the segments separated into their color group.

3. Choose 9 matching 2-1/2" x 6-1/2" spacers to pair with each group of matching 4-1/2" segments. Sew a spacer to the top of a 4-1/2" segment to complete a block. Repeat for each color group to make a total of 90 blocks.

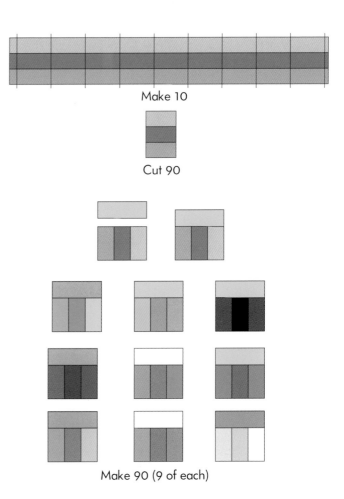

Make 10

Cut 90

Make 90 (9 of each)

Quilt Top Assembly

1. Referring to the Quilt Top Assembly Diagram, lay out the blocks, spacers and end spacers in 9 vertical rows. The even numbered rows begin with a block and end with a white 2-1/2" x 6-1/2" end spacer. Odd numbered rows begin with a white 2-1/2" x 6-1/2" end spacer and end with a block. Sew the pieces together in vertical rows.

2. Sew the vertical rows together to complete the quilt center. Press seams as each row is added.

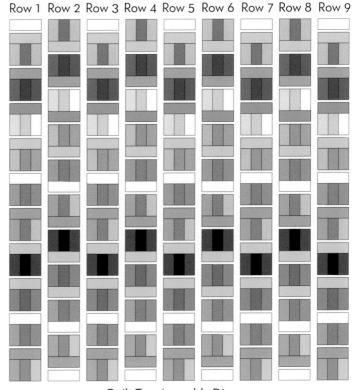

Row 1 Row 2 Row 3 Row 4 Row 5 Row 6 Row 7 Row 8 Row 9

Quilt Top Assembly Diagram

Finishing

1. Layer the quilt top, batting and backing.

2. Baste the layers together. Hand or machine quilt as desired. The featured quilt was quilted using a digitized design in an allover scroll design to complement the geometric design of the quilt.

3. Sew (7) 2-1/2" x WOF precut strips together along the short edges to make one continuous binding strip. Press seams open.

4. Press the strip in half lengthwise, wrong sides together, and sew to the raw edge of the quilt top. Fold binding over raw edges and hand stitch in place.

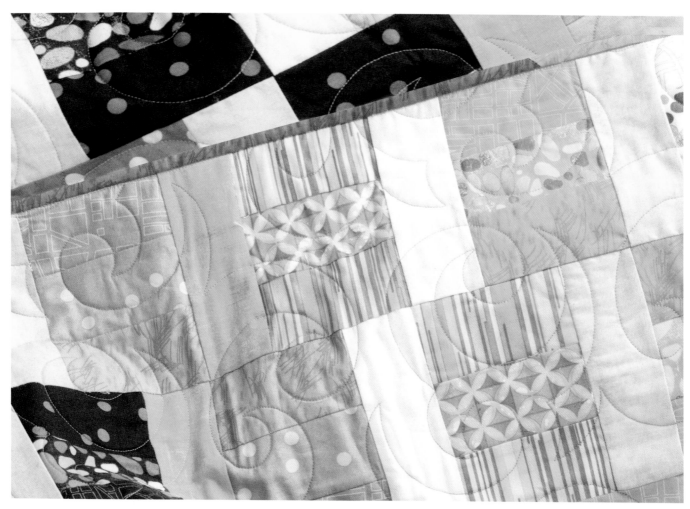

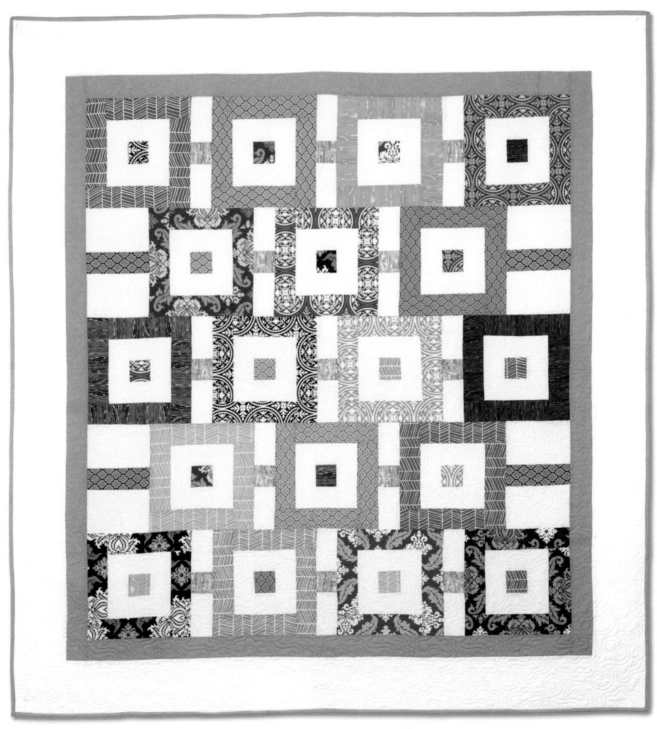

Quilt designed and pieced by Jean Ann Wright; longarm quilted by Sue Bentley
Longarm quilting design: Cloisonne by Patricia Ritter and Valerie Smith
Design Roll bundle: True Colors by Joel Dewberry for Free Spirit

Color Fusion Quilt

Jazz fusion was developed during the 1970's and 1980's. It is a musical genre that mixes jazz with rock and blues rhythms. Fusion allowed jazz musicians to blend the popularity of rock music with jazz and appeal to a larger listening audience.

Finished quilt size: 58" x 62"

Design Roll bundle = 2-1/2" x WOF strips

WOF = Width of fabric

NOTE: Sew with a scant 1/4" seam allowance

Fabric Requirements

- 1 design roll bundle of
  (20) 2-1/2" x WOF strips
- 1-1/2 yards white fabric
- 1 yard gray fabric
- 3-1/2 yards backing fabric
- Twin-size batting

Cutting

Separate the precut strips into 2 gray print strips and 18 color print strips.

From 1 gray print strip, cut:

(4) 2-1/2" x 6-1/2" rectangles for spacers

From 1 gray print strip, cut:

(13) 2-1/2" squares for spacers

From each (18) color print strip, cut:

(4) 2-1/2" x 8-1/2" rectangles for blocks

(1) 2-1/2" square for blocks.

From white fabric, cut:

(3) 4-1/2" x WOF strips. From the strips, cut:
    (8) 4-1/2" x 6-1/2" rectangles for spacers
    (26) 2-1/2" x 4-1/2" rectangles
      for spacers

(9) 2-1/2" x WOF strips. From the strips, cut:
    (72) 2-1/2" x 4-1/2" rectangles for blocks

(6) 4-1/2" x WOF strips. Sew the strips
    together end-to-end and cut:
    (2) 4-1/2" x 58-1/2" top/bottom
      outer border strips
    (2) 4-1/2" x 50-1/2" side outer
      border strips

From gray fabric, cut:

(6) 2-1/2" x WOF strips. Sew the strips
    together end-to-end and cut:
    (2) 2-1/2" x 44-3/4" top/bottom inner
      border strips
    (2) 2-1/2" x 52-1/2" side inner
      border strips

(6) 2-1/4" x WOF binding strips

Block and Spacer Assembly

1. Separate (4) 2-1/2" x 8-1/2" matching color print rectangles, (1) 2-1/2" contrasting color print square and (4) 2-1/2" x 4-1/2" white rectangles into a group. This group will make 1 block. Separate pieces into 18 groups.

2. Lay a 2-1/2" color print square on a 2-1/2" x 4-1/2" white rectangle, right sides together. Referring to the illustration, stitch a partial seam approximately 1-3/4" long.

3. Fold the square out and press seams toward the square to make unit A.

Unit A

4. Lay a 2-1/2" x 4-1/2" white rectangle on the adjacent side of unit A. Stitch the pieces together as shown. Press rectangle open to make unit B.

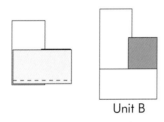

Unit B

5. Sew a 2-1/2" x 4-1/2" white rectangle to unit B as shown. Press rectangle open to make unit C.

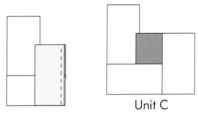

Unit C

6. Sew a 2-1/2" x 4-1/2" white rectangle to the remaining side of unit C taking care to fold the first rectangle away from the square as you stitch. (You do not want to catch it in the seam.) Press rectangle open.

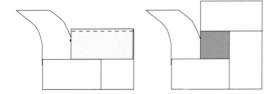

7. Fold the first rectangle over the square and the last rectangle you added. Finish sewing the partial seam to complete the block center. Press.

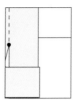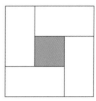

Block Center

8. In the same manner, sew the (4) 2-1/2" x 8-1/2" matching color print strips around the block center to complete the block. Make a total of 18 blocks.

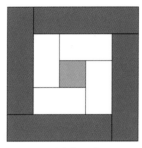

Make 18

9. Sew 2-1/2" x 4-1/2" white rectangles to opposite sides of a 2-1/2" gray print square to make a narrow spacer. Make 13 narrow spacers.

Make 13

10. Sew 4-1/2" x 6-1/2" white rectangles to opposite sides of a 2-1/2" x 6-1/2" gray print strip to make a wide spacer unit. Make 4 wide spacers.

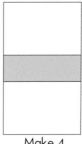

Make 4

Quilt Assembly

1. Referring to the Quilt Assembly Diagram, lay out the blocks, narrow and wide spacers in 5 horizontal rows.

2. Sew the pieces together in rows. Sew the rows together to complete the quilt center. Press seams as each row is added.

Adding the Borders

1. Sew the 2-1/2" x 44-3/4" gray top/bottom inner border strips to the top and bottom of the quilt top. Sew the 2-1/2" x 52-1/2" gray side inner border strips to opposite sides of the quilt top. Press seams toward borders.

2. Sew the 4-1/2" x 58-1/2" white side outer border strips to the top and bottom of the quilt top. Sew the 4-1/2" x 50-1/2" white top/bottom outer border strips to opposite sides of the quilt top. Press seams toward borders to compete the quilt top.

Finishing

1. Layer the quilt top, batting and backing.

2. Baste the layers together. Hand or machine quilt as desired. The featured quilt was quilted using a gently curving quilt design that complemented the classic designs in the design roll.

3. Sew the (6) 2-1/4" x WOF binding strips together along the short edges to make one continuous binding strip. Press seams open.

4. Press the strip in half lengthwise, wrong sides together, and sew to the raw edge of the quilt top. Fold binding over raw edges and hand stitch in place.

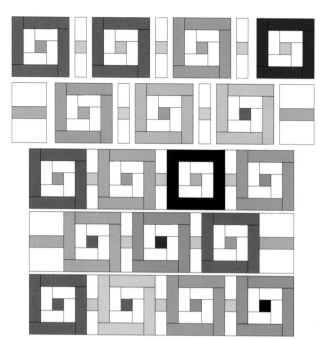

Quilt Assembly Diagram

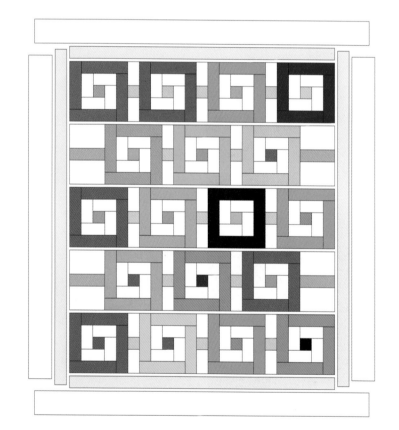

Quilt designed and pieced by Jean Ann Wright; longarm quilted by Sue Bentley
Design Roll bundle: Kaffe Fassett Classics by Kaffe Fassett for Westminster Rowan

Finished quilt size: 74" x 86"
Design Roll bundle = 2-1/2" x WOF strips
WOF = Width of fabric
NOTE: Sew with a scant 1/4" seam allowance

Fabric Requirements

- 2 design roll bundles of
  (30) 2-1/2" x WOF strips
- 2-1/4 yards white fabric
- 5/8 yard print fabric
- 5-1/4 yards backing fabric
- Full-size batting
- Template material
- Optional: Hexagon Trim Tool
  by Creative Grids®

Cutting

From template material, cut:
Partial hexagon template on page 23

From **each** precut strip, cut:

(7) partial hexagon pieces using the partial
hexagon template, ruler and rotary
cutter. You will have a total of 420
partial hexagon pieces.

NOTE: Use the template to position your
ruler for cutting. Do not cut around the
template without a ruler. Do not stack
more than 6 strips when cutting.

Partial Hexagon Cutting

From white fabric, cut:

(10) 2-1/2" x WOF strips
Sew pairs of strips together end-to-
end to make 5 sashing strips.

(8) 5-1/2" x WOF border strips
Sew pairs of strips together
end-to-end to make 4 border strips.
Border strips will be trimmed to size in
Adding the Borders.

From print fabric, cut:

(9) 2-1/4" x WOF binding strips

Gypsy Jazz Quilt

Gypsy jazz, also known as gypsy swing or hot club jazz, originated in France where many of the musicians worked in Paris in ensembles. The Musette-style waltz is a precursor to gypsy jazz and remains an important component. It combines a dark gypsy musical flavor with the bright swing music popular in the 1930's. The Gypsy Jazz quilt has the flavor of dark and bright as the partial hexagons swing in colorful rows.

Row Assembly

1. Separate the partial hexagon pieces into 6 sets with 70 pieces in each set.

2. Referring to the diagrams, place two partial hexagon pieces right sides together as shown. Sew the pieces together along the short angled edge and press open.

3. Referring to the diagram, place another partial hexagon on the piece from step 2, right sides together along one long edge. Sew the pieces together and press open.

4. Continue sewing the partial hexagon pieces one at a time in this manner until all 70 pieces are sewn in place to complete 1 partial hexagon row. Make a total of 6 partial hexagon rows.

5. Referring to the diagram, use a straight edge ruler and rotary cutter to trim the top and bottom of each row.

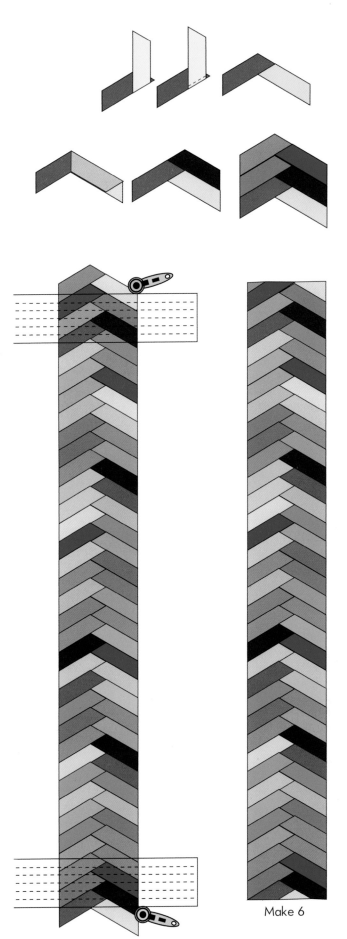

Make 6

20

Quilt Center Assembly

1. Measure each row from top to bottom. This measurement may vary slightly due to the fact some seams are stitched on the bias. Choose a measurement that is in the middle range and use this measurement to cut the (5) 2-1/2" sashing strips to size. The measurement should be approximately 75" to 76".

2. Referring to the Quilt Assembly Diagram, lay out the partial hexagon rows and the sashing strips as shown.

3. Sew the pieces together to complete the quilt center. Press seams toward the sashing strips. Square up the quilt center if necessary.

Quilt Assembly Diagram

Adding the Borders

1. Trim 2 border strips to the same length as the sashing strips in step 1 of Quilt Center Assembly on page 21 to make the side borders.

2. Sew the side borders to opposite sides of the quilt center. Press seams toward the borders.

3. Measure the quilt center from side to side across the center. Include the side borders in this measurement. Cut the remaining 2 border strips to this measurement to make the top/bottom borders.

4. Sew the top/bottom borders to the top and bottom of the quilt center to complete the quilt top. Press seams toward the borders.

Finishing

1. Layer the quilt top, batting and backing.

2. Baste the layers together. Hand or machine quilt as desired. The featured quilt was quilted using a braid design in the sashing and borders and a meandering design in the partial hexagon rows.

3. Sew (9) 2-1/4" x WOF binding strips together along the short ends to make one continuous binding strip. Press seams open.

4. Press the strip in half lengthwise, wrong sides together, and sew to the raw edge of the quilt top. Fold binding over raw edges and hand stitch in place.

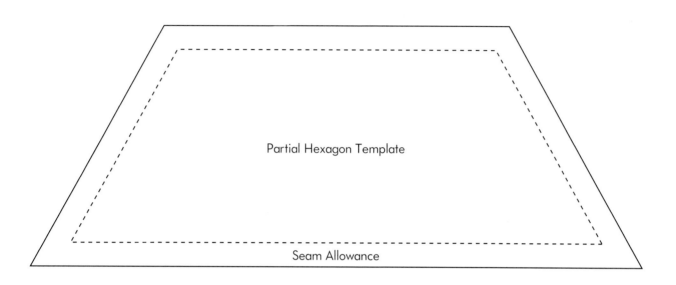

Partial Hexagon Template

Seam Allowance

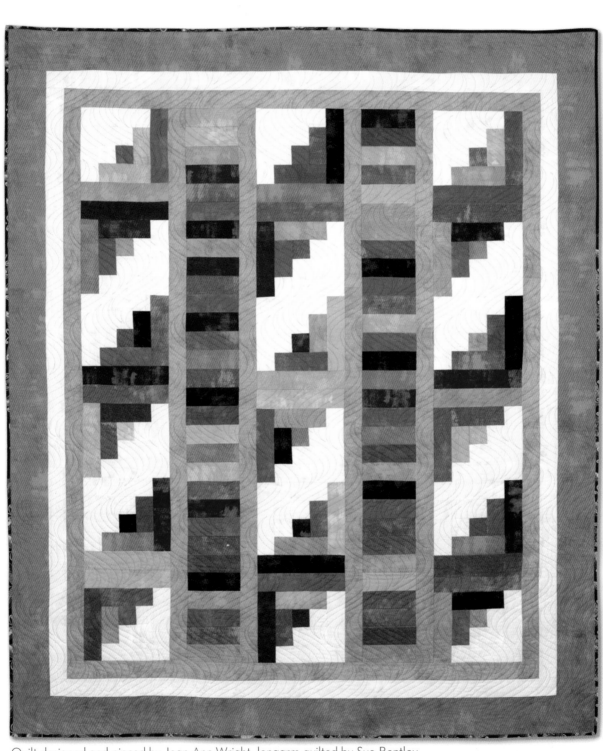

Quilt designed and pieced by Jean Ann Wright; longarm quilted by Sue Bentley
Longarm quilting design: Curvy Weave by Karen Thompson
Jelly Roll bundle and additional fabrics: Grunge Basics by BasicGrey for Moda

Finished quilt size: 66" x 76"
Jelly Roll bundle = 2-1/2" x WOF strips
WOF = Width of fabric
NOTE: Sew with a scant 1/4" seam allowance

Fabric Requirements

- 1 jelly roll bundle of
  (40) 2-1/2" x WOF strips
- 1-1/2 yards white fabric
- 1 yard gray fabric
- 1 yard orange fabric
- 2/3 yard print fabric
- 4-3/4 yards backing fabric
- Full-size batting

Cutting

NOTE: Use a random assortment of precut strips to achieve more variety in your blocks.

From precut strips, cut a total of:

(18) 2-1/2" center squares

(18) 2-1/2" x 4-1/2" strips

(18) 2-1/2" x 6-1/2" strips

(18) 2-1/2" x 8-1/2" strips

(18) 2-1/2" x 10-1/2" strips

From remaining precut strips, cut:

(60) 2-1/2" x 6-1/2" strips
    for the pieced strip rows

From white fabric, cut:

(18) 2-1/2" squares

(18) 2-1/2" x 4-1/2" strips

(18) 2-1/2" x 6-1/2" strips

(18) 2-1/2" x 8-1/2" strips

(7) 2-1/2" x WOF strips. Sew the strips
    together end-to-end and cut:
    (2) 2-1/2" x 64-1/2" side middle
        border strips
    (2) 2-1/2" x 56-1/2" top/bottom
        middle border strips

Let's Swing Quilt

Swing music was developed in the early 1930's and became a distinctive style of its own by 1940. Swing's popularity was due in part to its very danceable rhythm. Swing dancing is still in vogue today with many dancing partners participating in competitions.

From gray fabric, cut:
(12) 2-1/2" x WOF strips. Sew the strips
    together end-to-end and cut:
    (4) 2-1/2" x 60-1/2" sashing strips
    (2) 2-1/2" x 60-1/2" side inner
        border strips
    (2) 2-1/2" x 54-1/2" top/bottom
        inner border strips

From orange fabric, cut:
(8) 4-1/2" x WOF strips. Sew the strips
    together end-to-end and cut:
    (2) 4-1/2" x 68-1/2" side
        outer borders
    (2) 4-1/2" x 66-1/2" top/bottom
        outer borders

From print fabric, cut:
(8) 2-1/4" x WOF binding strips

Block and Row Assembly

1. Referring to the diagram, lay out (1) 2-1/2" color center square, (1) 2-1/2" white square, (2) 2-1/2" x 4-1/2" color and white strips, (2) 2-1/2" x 6-1/2" color and white strips, (2) 2-1/2" x 8-1/2" color and white strips and (1) 2-1/2" x 10-1/2" color strip.

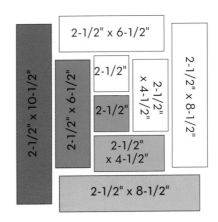

2. Following the diagram sew the pieces around the center square in the sequence shown to make a Log Cabin block. Press the seams as each piece is added. Make a total of 18 Log Cabin blocks.

3. Referring to the Quilt Assembly Diagram on page 27, lay out the Log Cabin blocks in 3 vertical rows with 6 blocks in each row. Note the orientation of the blocks within each row. Sew the blocks together in rows.

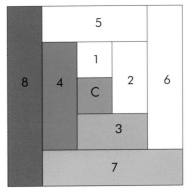

Make 18

4. Lay out (30) 2-1/2" x 6-1/2" color strips in random order. Sew the strips together to complete a pieced row. Make a total of 2 pieced rows.

5. Sew a 2-1/2" x 60-1/2" gray sashing strip to opposite sides of the pieced rows. Press seams toward sashing.

Make 2

Quilt Center Assembly

1. Referring to the Quilt Assembly Diagram, lay out the 3 blocks rows and 2 pieced rows.

2. Sew the rows together to complete the quilt center. Press seams toward sashing.

Quilt Assembly Diagram

Adding the Borders

1. Sew the 2-1/2" x 60-1/2" gray side inner border strips to opposite sides of the quilt center. Press seams toward borders.

2. Sew the 2-1/2" x 54-1/2" gray top/bottom inner border strips to the top/bottom of the quilt center. Press seams toward borders.

3. Sew the 2-1/2" x 64-1/2" white side middle border strips to opposite sides of the quilt center. Press seams toward borders.

4. Sew the 2-1/2" x 56-1/2" white top/bottom middle border strips to the top/bottom of the quilt center. Press seams toward borders.

5. Sew the 4-1/2" x 68-1/2" orange side outer border strips to opposite sides of the quilt center. Press seams toward borders.

6. Sew the 4-1/2" x 66-1/2" orange top/bottom outer border strips to the top/bottom of the quilt center. Press seams toward borders to complete the quilt top.

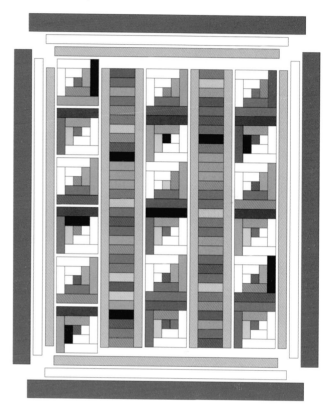

Finishing

1. Layer the quilt top, batting and backing.

2. Baste the layers together. Hand or machine quilt as desired. The featured quilt was quilted in a swinging design to emphasize the up and down movement in the vertical rows of color.

3. Sew (8) 2-1/4" x WOF binding strips together along the short ends to make one continuous binding strip. Press seams open.

4. Press the strip in half lengthwise, wrong sides together, and sew to the raw edge of the quilt top. Fold binding over raw edges and hand stitch in place.

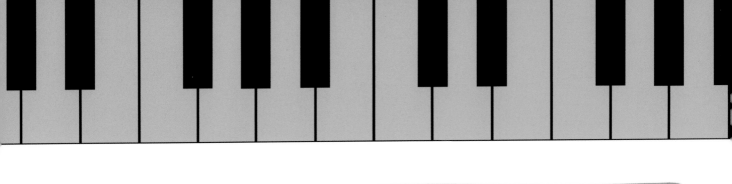

Quilt designed and pieced by Jean Ann Wright; longarm quilted by Sue Bentley
Longarm quilting design: Seamless by Sarah Ann Myers
Jelly Roll bundle: One for You, One for Me by Pat Sloan for Moda

Ragtime Quilt

Ragtime, a musical style popular between 1895 and 1918, has a syncopated or "ragged" rhythm. It was a modification of the marching music made popular by John Philip Sousa. Ragtime, which fell out of favor when jazz became popular, has experienced many revivals since it was rediscovered in the mid-twentieth century. This scrappy-looking quilt has a ragged appearance with its different strip sizes, fabric combinations and random block placement.

Finished quilt size: 62" x 72"
Jelly Roll bundle = 2-1/2" x WOF strips
WOF = Width of fabric
NOTE: Sew with a scant 1/4" seam allowance

Fabric Requirements

• 1 jelly roll bundle of
   (40) 2-1/2" x WOF strips

• 1-1/4 yards border fabric

• 1/2 yard orange fabric

• 4-1/2 yards backing fabric

• Twin-size batting

Cutting

From **each** of 10 precut strips, cut:
(4) 2-1/2" x 10-1/2" strips
    for a total of 40 strips

From **each** of 5 precut strips, cut:
(1) 2-1/2" square for a total of 5 squares

(3) 2-1/2" x 10-1/2" strips
    for a total of 15 strips

From border fabric, cut:
(6) 6-1/2" x WOF strips. Sew the strips
    together end-to-end and cut:
    (2) 6-1/2" x 60-1/2" side border strips
    (2) 6-1/2" x 62-1/2" top/bottom
        border strips

From orange fabric, cut:
(6) 2-1/4" x WOF binding strips

Block Assembly

1. Divide the remaining 25 precut strips into 5 groups with 5 strips in each group.

2. Sew the strips in each group together along the long edges to make a strip set. Press seams. Make a total of 5 strip sets.

3. Cut each strip set into (6) 6-1/2" segments and (1) 2-1/2" segment as shown. You should have a total of (30) 6-1/2" segments and (5) 2-1/2" segments.

4. Sew the (5) 2-1/2" squares together in a row and set aside with the other 2-1/2" segments.

5. Lay out (2) 2-1/2" x 10-1/2" strips and (1) 6-1/2" segment. Sew the pieces together as shown to make Block A. Make a total of 18 Block A.

6. Lay out (2) 2-1/2" x 10-1/2" strips and (1) 6-1/2" segment. Sew the pieces together as shown to make Block B. Make a total of 6 Block B.

7. Lay out (1) 2-1/2" segment, (1) 2-1/2" x 10-1/2" strip and (1) 6-1/2" segment. Sew the pieces together as shown to make Block C. Make a total of 6 Block C.

8. Trim all the blocks to 10-1/2" square.

Quilt Center Assembly

1. Referring to the Quilt Center Assembly Diagram, lay out the blocks in 6 horizontal rows with 5 blocks in each row. Sew the blocks together in rows.

2. Sew the rows together to complete the quilt center. Press seams as each row is added.

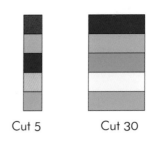

Cut 5   Cut 30

Block A-Make 18

Block B-Make 6

Block C-Make 6

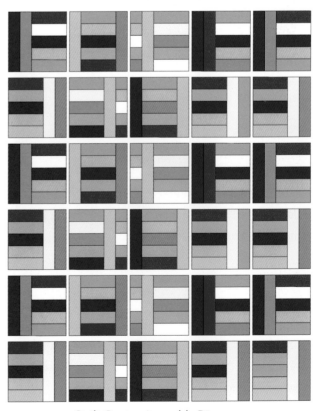

Quilt Center Assembly Diagram

Adding the Borders

1. Sew the 6-1/2" x 60-1/2" side border strips to opposite sides of the quilt center. Press seams toward borders.

2. Sew the 6-1/2" x 62-1/2" top/bottom border strips to the top/bottom of the quilt center. Press seams toward borders to complete the quilt top.

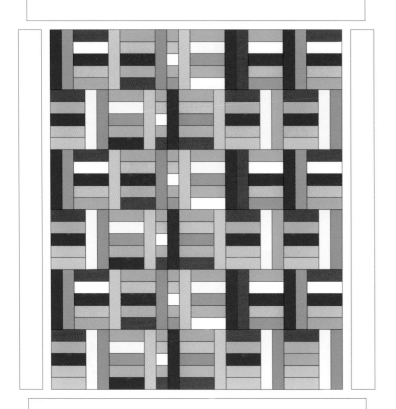

Finishing

1. Layer the quilt top, batting and backing.

2. Baste the layers together. Hand or machine quilt as desired. The featured quilt was quilted using a simple meandering design.

3. Sew (6) 2-1/4" x WOF binding strips together along the short ends to make one continuous binding strip. Press seams open.

4. Press the strip in half lengthwise, wrong sides together, and sew to the raw edge of the quilt top. Fold binding over raw edges and hand stitch in place.

Quilt designed and pieced by Jean Ann Wright; longarm quilted by Sue Bentley
Longarm quilting designs: Floralish by Barbara Becker and Hexi by Joyce Lundrigan
Jelly Roll bundle: Simple Mark's Summer by Malka Dubrawsky for Moda

Hex-A-Dizzy Quilt

South Carolina native Dizzy Gillespie is one of the best known names in jazz music. He experimented with jazz to create his own unique style. Gillespie was known for clowning around, leaving a legacy of goodwill as he traveled the globe serving as an international musical ambassador. The featured quilt has hexagon blocks that seem to spin leaving the viewer dizzy.

Finished quilt size: 56" x 73"
Jelly Roll bundle = 2-1/2" x WOF strips
WOF = Width of fabric
NOTE: Sew with a scant 1/4" seam allowance

Fabric Requirements

- 1 jelly roll bundle of
  (40) 2-1/2" x WOF strips

- 2 yards white fabric

- 1/2 yard print fabric

- 5 yards backing fabric

- Full-size batting

- Template material

- Optional: T-60 ruler by Creative Grids®

Cutting

Separate the precut strips into 13 groups with 3 strips in each group. You will have 1 extra strip.

From template material, cut:

Half-triangle template on page 37

Triangle template on page 38

From white fabric, cut:

(6) 6-1/2" x WOF strips
　　From the strips, cut:
　　40 setting triangles using the triangle template, ruler and rotary cutter

　　From 8 setting triangles, cut:
　　16 half-setting triangles using the half-triangle template, ruler and rotary cutter

NOTE: Use the template to position your ruler for cutting. Do not cut around the template without a ruler.

(7) 4-1/2" x WOF strips. Sew the strips together end-to-end and cut:
　　(2) 4-1/2" x 65-1/2" side border strips
　　(2) 4-1/2" x 56-1/2" top/bottom
　　　　border strips

From print fabric, cut:

(7) 2-1/4" x WOF binding strips

Block Assembly

1. Sew the 3 precut strips in each group together along the long edges to make a strip set. Press seams open. Make a total of 13 strip sets.

Make 13

2. Using the triangle template, cut a total of 120 triangles from the strip sets as shown.

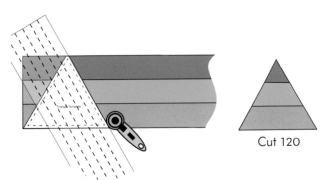

Cut 120

3. Lay out 2 sets of 3 matching triangles alternating the triangles as shown.

4. Sew the triangles together in sets of 3 to make a half-hexagon. Sew the half-hexagons together to complete a Hexagon Block A. Make a total of 14 Hexagon Block A.

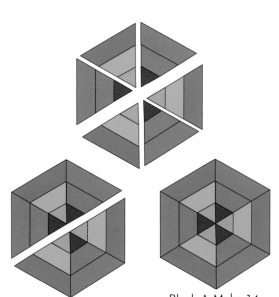

Block A-Make 14

5. Lay out 3 sets of 2 matching triangles as shown.

6. Sew the triangles together in sets of 3 to make a half-hexagon. Sew the half-hexagons together to complete a Hexagon Block B. Make a total of 6 Hexagon Block B.

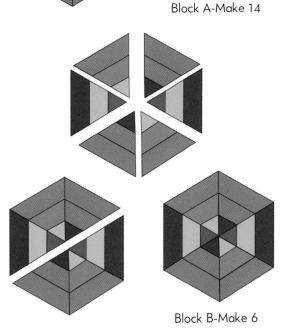

Block B-Make 6

Quilt Center Assembly

1. Referring to the Row Assembly Diagram, lay out 4 vertical rows with 5 hexagon blocks, 8 setting triangles and 4 half-setting triangles in each row. Mix hexagon blocks A and B in any manner you wish.

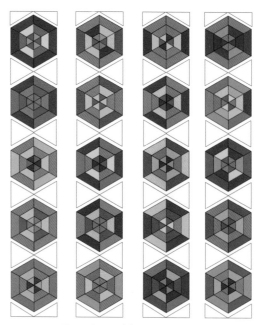

Row Assembly Diagram

2. Sew the hexagon blocks and setting triangles together. Press seams.

3. Sew the pieces together in rows.

4. Sew the half-setting triangles to the top and bottom of each row.

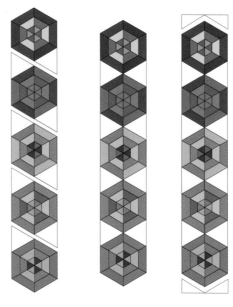

4. Sew the rows together to complete the quilt center.

Adding the Borders

1. Referring to the Quilt Assembly Diagram, sew the (2) white 4-1/2" x 65-1/2" side borders to opposite sides of the quilt top. Press seams toward borders.

2. Sew the (2) 4-1/2" x 56-1/2" white top/bottom borders to the top and bottom of the quilt center to complete the quilt top.

Finishing

1. Layer the quilt top, batting and backing.

2. Baste the layers together. Hand or machine quilt as desired. The featured quilt was quilted using two designs; one in the blocks and another in the setting triangles and borders.

3. Sew (7) 2-1/4" x WOF binding strips together along the short ends to make one continuous binding strip. Press seams open.

4. Press the strip in half lengthwise, wrong sides together, and sew to the raw edge of the quilt top. Fold binding over raw edges and hand stitch in place.

Quilt Assembly Diagram

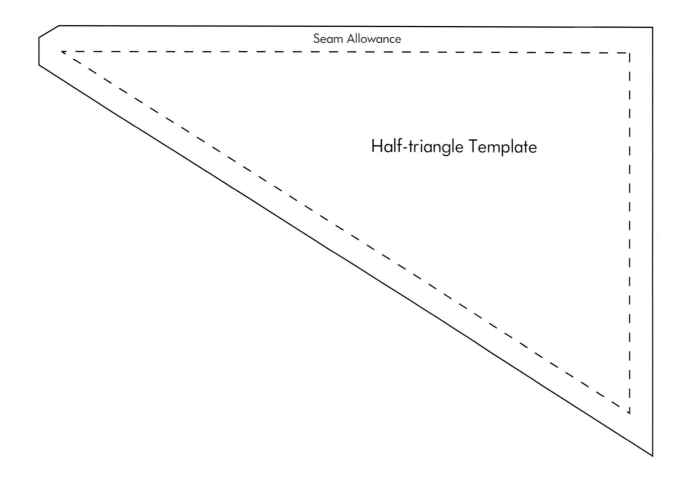

Seam Allowance

Half-triangle Template

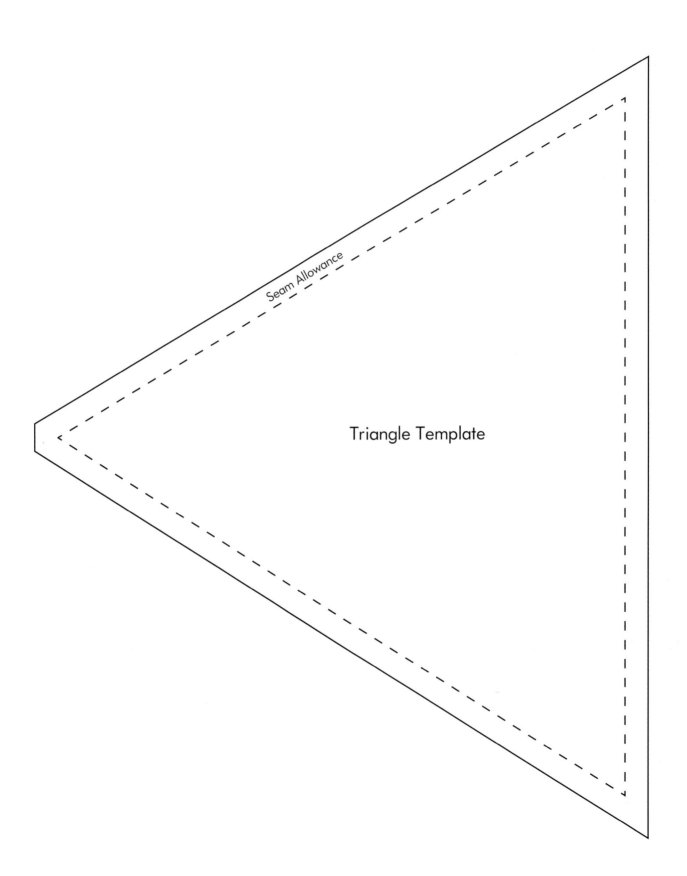

Seam Allowance

Triangle Template

Quilt designed and pieced by Jean Ann Wright; longarm quilted by Robin Kinley
Sushi Roll bundle: Carnival Batik by Mirah

Syncopation Quilt

In music, syncopation is made up of a variety of unexpected and offbeat rhythms. The Syncopation quilt is inspired by a needlework design known as bargello. The bargello design has colors going up and down in a syncopated design as they move from one side of the quilt to the other.

Finished quilt size: 44" x 52"
Sushi Roll bundle = 2-1/2" x WOF strips
WOF = Width of fabric
NOTE: Sew with a scant 1/4" seam allowance

Fabric Requirements

- 1 sushi roll bundle of
  (24) 2-1/2" x WOF strips
- 1 yard white fabric
- 1/3 yard teal fabric
- 2 yards backing fabric
- Craft-size batting

Cutting

From precut strips:
Refer to the chart to cut the number/size of segments in the colors shown.

NOTE: For reference, 1 precut strip will yield (17) 2-1/2" squares OR
(9) 2-1/2" x 4-1/2" pieces OR
(6) 2-1/2" x 6-1/2" pieces.

From white fabric, cut:
(5) 5-1/2" x WOF strips
Sew the strips together end-to-end and cut:
(2) 5-1/2" x 42-1/2" side border strips
(2) 5-1/2" x 46-1/2" top/bottom strips

From teal fabric, cut:
(5) 2-1/4" x WOF binding strips

Cutting Chart

4 strips Cut 34 — 4-1/2"	Cut 2 — 6-1/2"	Cut 12 — 2-1/2"
4 strips Cut 34 — 4-1/2"	Cut 3 — 2-1/2"	Cut 4 — 4-1/2"
4 strips Cut 34 — 4-1/2"	Cut 18 — 2-1/2"	Cut 4 — 6-1/2"
4 strips Cut 28 — 4-1/2"	Cut 2 — 2-1/2"	
4 strips Cut 18 — 4-1/2"	Cut 4 — 6-1/2"	

Row and Quilt Center Assembly

1. Referring to the Sewing the Rows Diagram, lay out the pieces for each row. Sew the pieces together in rows. Label the rows as you sew them together.

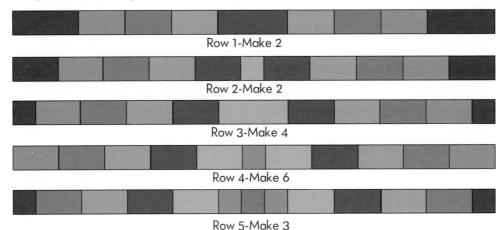

Row 1-Make 2

Row 2-Make 2

Row 3-Make 4

Row 4-Make 6

Row 5-Make 3

Sewing the Rows Diaagram

2. Referring to the Quilt Center Assembly Diagram, sew the rows together in the order shown to complete the quilt center. Press the seams as you add each row.

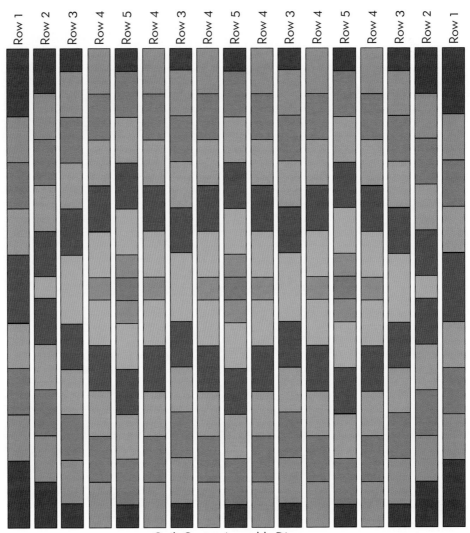

Quilt Center Assembly Diagram

Adding the Borders

1. Sew the 5-1/2" x 42-1/2" white side borders to opposite sides of the quilt center. Press seams toward the borders.

2. Sew the 5-1/2" x 46-1/2" white top/bottom borders to the top/bottom of the quilt center to complete the quilt top. Press seams toward the borders.

Finishing

1. Layer the quilt top, batting and backing.

2. Baste the layers together. Hand or machine quilt as desired. The featured quilt was quilted using a large floral design to emphasize the blue and yellow centers created when the rows came together. These were expanded with spirals into the borders and finished with small flowers and leaves.

3. Sew (5) 2-1/4" x WOF binding strips together along the short ends to make one continuous binding strip. Press seams open.

4. Press the strip in half lengthwise, wrong sides together, and sew to the raw edge of the quilt top. Fold binding over raw edges and hand stitch in place.

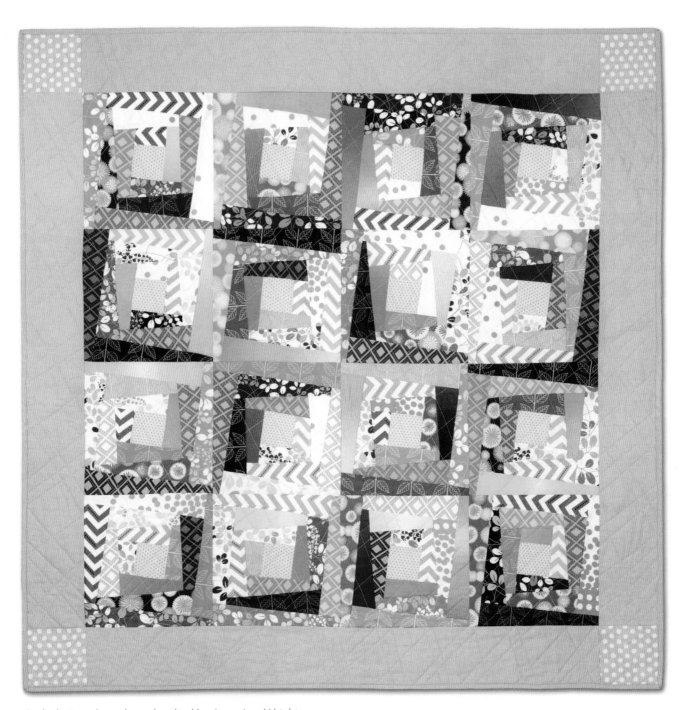

Quilt designed, made and quilted by Jean Ann Wright

Pick Up Sticks Quilt

A jazz drummer is influenced by many individual drummers and the styles that reflect where they have lived, whether New Orleans, the Caribbean or Africa. A gradual "freeing" of the beat has emerged over time. The 16 blocks in this quilt has a series of "sticks" or strips around the center square that are randomly trimmed so no two strips are exactly the same size or shape.

Finished quilt size: 48" x 48"
Precut bundle = 2-1/2" x WOF strips
WOF = Width of fabric
NOTE: Sew with a scant 1/4" seam allowance

Fabric Requirements

- 1 precut bundle of
  (40) 2-1/2" x WOF strips

- 1/4 yard gray small dot fabric

- 1/8 yard gray large dot fabric

- 1 yard gray fabric

- 3 yards backing fabric

- Twin-size batting

Cutting

Separate the precut strips into light and dark color groups. The strips will be cut the length needed when making the blocks.

From gray small dot fabric, cut:

(2) 3-1/2" x WOF strips
    From the strips, cut:
    (16) 3-1/2" center squares

From gray large dot fabric, cut:

(4) 4-1/2" squares for cornerstones

From gray fabric, cut:

(4) 4-1/2" x 40-1/2" border strips

(5) 2-1/4" x WOF binding strips

Block Assembly

Precut strips are sewn around a center square and trimmed at random angles to create the block.

1. Sew a 2-1/2" light precut strip to one side of a 3-1/2" gray small dot center square. Trim the strip approximately 1" longer than the center square.

2. Sew another light precut strip to the center square overlapping the first strip and extending approximately 1" past the end of the strip.

3. In the same manner, sew dark precut strips to the remaining sides of the center square.

4. Trim the unit to 5-1/2" square using a ruler and rotary cutter. Position the ruler at random angles when cutting.

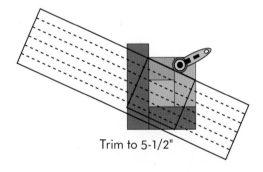

Trim to 5-1/2"

5. Repeat steps 1-3 to sew an additional four precut strips around the center square. Trim the unit to 8" square.

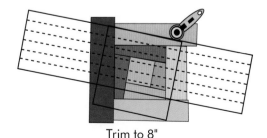

Trim to 8"

6. Repeat steps 1-3 to sew an additional four precut strips around the center square. Trim the unit to 10-1/2" square to complete a block. Make a total of 16 blocks.

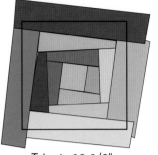
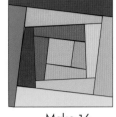

Make 16

Trim to 10-1/2"

Quilt Center Assembly

1. Sew the blocks together in sets of four. The two dark sides in each block should be positioned on the outer edges with the light sides meeting in the center of the set. Make a total of four block sets.

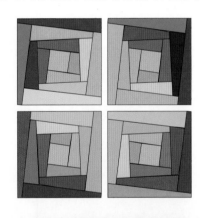

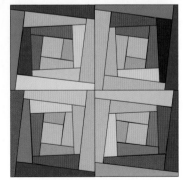

Make 4

2. Referring to the Quilt Center Assembly Diagram, lay out the four block sets. Sew the sets together to complete the quilt center.

Adding the Borders

1. Sew a 4-1/2" x 40-1/2" gray border strip to opposite sides of the quilt center. Press seams toward borders.

2. Sew a 4-1/2" gray large dot cornerstone to opposite short edges of the remaining border strips to complete top/bottom borders.

3. Sew the top/bottom borders to the top and bottom of the quilt center to complete the quilt top.

Finishing

1. Layer the quilt top, batting and backing.

2. Baste the layers together. Hand or machine quilt as desired. The featured quilt was quilted using a series of long, straight stitching in irregular widths from top to bottom.

3. Sew (5) 2-1/4" x WOF binding strips together along the short edges to make one continuous binding strip. Press seams open.

4. Press the strip in half lengthwise, wrong sides together, and sew to the raw edge of the quilt top. Fold binding over raw edges and hand stitch in place.

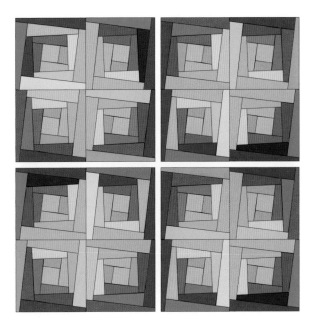

Quilt Center Assembly Diagram

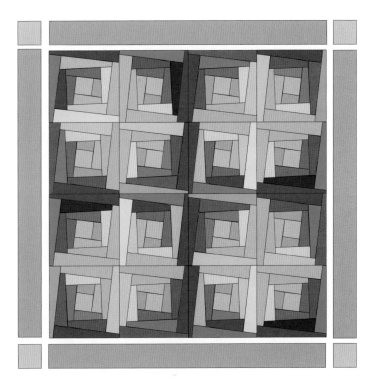